THE ROLE OF THE PROJECT MANAGER

THE ROLE OF THE PROJECT MANAGER

John McManus

The Role of ... Series
Best Practice Management Reports

Technical Communications (Publishing) Limited

ISBN 1 85953 090 7

Technical Communications (Publishing) Ltd.
PO Box 6
Hitchin
Hertfordshire SG5 2DB
England

Telephone/Fax: (01462) 437075

Printed in England

Contents

Foreword

There are many books about project management, the majority of which assist the reader in how to manage projects and provide an insight into the techniques and procedures of project management.

Each of us have our own favourites and disappointments. Most of them also contain a few pages on the role of a project manager but in my view these never tend to go far enough.

This book is different. It focuses on what the project manager does, what skills they need and how they can continue their training and development.

Chapter one puts projects into context. Chapter two considers the key role of the project manager. Namely, the need to manage the project team and concentrates on developing relationships between all the key project team members.

Chapter three is on Competencies and I was particularly pleased to see this, having been involved in some of the early work on the development of competencies on behalf of The Association of Project Managers. I am sure that with the trend towards competence based assessments like NVQs, this will become an increasingly important element in every professional's life.

Chapter four covers Training and Development and again I think as professionals we should try to maintain our knowledge and there are some useful hints within this chapter.

The final chapter actually looks at managing projects.

I think the main value of the book will be for people contemplating a career in project management, or others considering the role of project managers within their organisation. It is not a book on how to manage projects.

Richard Pharro
MANAGING DIRECTOR APM GROUP LIMITED.

Acknowledgements

In the preparation of this report I would like to thank Gordon Napier of the Royal Institution of Chartered Surveyors (QS Division) for reading the manuscript and making some very helpful suggestions; also to Alan Osborne (Group Safety Director, BAA) for his helpful comments to earlier drafts of this document; and to Jennifer Cawkwell, Central Nottingham Healthcare (NHS) Trust who masterminded the complexities of Project Management and contributed to Chapter 2. I would also like to thank the Association of Project Managers for their assistance and permission to use copyright material from their publication the *Body of Knowledge*.

To my friend (and former mentor) Dr Andrew Campbell for his encouragement and enthusiasm (don't leave it too long next time). To the late Professor Jack Burbidge for the knowledge he passed on to me – he is sadly missed. Finally I would like to thank Dr Glyn Jones who acted as catalyst and supported this project – thank you.

To the following people who live it 260 days a year: Paul Atmore, Max Batten, Alec Bruty, Mandy Cook, Alan Holmes, John Horan, Liz Shedden, Brian Taylor, Vince Tooke and Charles Virr.

J. J. McManus

About the author

A professional mechanical/production engineer with postgraduate qualifications in industrial management and business administration, John McManus began his career in 1976, gaining experience with a number of European blue chip companies. After a short academic sabbatical in the USA, he returned to the UK, working as a manufacturing consultant advising organisations on Terotechnology, Group Technology and MRP II. His clients included Philips International, Philips UK and GEC.

John currently works in the transport sector, managing the implementation of Information Technology Systems. His research interests cover Total Quality Management (TQM) and Business Process Re-engineering. He is the author/co-author of three books including *Resisting Change* and *An Implementation Guide on How to Re-engineer Your Business.*

In addition to his books, John has authored 30 papers on TQM and other management related topics which have been published in several languages (English, French, and Japanese). He is also a sought after speaker on TQM in Europe. In 1994 John was short listed for the Chair, Professor of Business and Business English at the Technical University (Fachhochschule Für Technik und Wirtschaft), Reutlingen, in Germany.

The author is a participating member of several committees, including the International Organisation of Management (Geneva) Strategy Unit, Networking For Industry and the all-party Parliament Manufacturing Interest Group.

John McManus lives in the market town of Newark and can be contacted through the publishers.

1 The emergence of the project organisation

The success or otherwise of an organisation is directly related to its market share and profits. Parenthetically, many organisations in the UK and Western Europe are now restructuring their operations and business processes to deliver products and services within a cost-effective project management structure (the meaning of the term project organisation is discussed below.)

A decade ago, project-managed organisations were a rarity; today, they can be found in all sectors of industry and commerce, including construction, engineering, information technology, banking, communications and many others. The growth in project-managed organisations is in part attributed to the social changes that have taken place, resulting in the recognition that giving managers responsibility and freedom to exercise initiative increases their motivation and performance.

Functional vs. Project Organisations

Traditionally, organisations have been structured (and to some extent still are) by function and task specialisation. In such organisations, people have well defined jobs and a place on an organisational chart, where everybody knows exactly what to do. Within the last few years, however, there has been a move away from traditional *functional structures* to flatter, more compact compositions which serve the individual customer and client needs.

Customers (i.e. those who pay for goods and services) expect organisations to compete not solely on price but also on quality and responsiveness to customer demand (i.e. speed of delivery to market).

An Overview of Functional Organisations

Functional organisations, as illustrated in Figure 1.1, are characterised by bureaucratic management where decisions are made at the centre. Such structures are based on task specialisation (one person one job), which usually result in a low adaptive response both within the organisation and within its environment. Authority is based on the manager–subordinate concept where middle management (Level Four) authority is limited.

Level One	Managing Director
Level Two	Functional Directors
Level Three	Department Heads
Level Four	Subordinates (all grades)

Figure 1.1 Example of a functional organisation structure

Functional organisations are, essentially, pyramids with four chains of command. In actuality there may, of course, be other functions and levels depending on the size of the organisation, the complexity of the product(s) and the technology employed. Structures such as this tend to be heavily centralised, i.e. major

decisions are taken at the top, either by the board or by the directors. In such circumstances, senior management alone (i.e. Levels One and Two) are responsible for achieving the economic objectives of the organisation.

As functional organisations increase in size and complexity, problems arise: strain on the control and internal communication systems create physical and non-physical barriers (Table 1.1) which eventually lead to loss of performance and efficiency.

Functional organisations adhere too much to the principles of specialisation; such an emphasis can become a weakness where technology, work roles and market requirements interact. What is needed is an organisational structure which exploits individual competency-based skills: to deliver efficient, economic products and services of world class quality – the *project organisation*.

Table 1.1 Physical and non-physical barriers in organisations

- Poor Internal Communications (verbal and written)
- Senior Management – no feeling of mutual trust
- No Emphasis on Team Building
- Poor Employee Morale – lack of employee motivation
- Lack of Information Sharing ('need to know' mentality)
- Lack of Social Responsibility
- Lack of Empathy with Customers (internal and external)
- Lack of Employee Empowerment
- Quality and Competence of Decision Makers
- Lack of Coherent Infrastructure for Employee Development

Project Organisations

So how does the project organisation differ from the functional organisation? In essence, project organisations remove many of the barriers identified in Table 1.1, by creating an environment which supports, encourages and rewards staff at all levels.

Research undertaken by Peters and Waterman (1982) for their book *In Search of Excellence* identified eight attributes which high performance companies share, at least four of these attributes are to be found within project organisations. They are:

1.   **Staying close to the customer:** learning his or her preferences and catering for them.

2.   **Productivity through people:** creating in all employees the awareness that their best efforts are essential and that they will share in the rewards of the company's success.

3.   **Simple form, lean staff:** few administration layers, few people at the upper levels.

4.   **Hands-on, value driven:** insisting that management keep in touch with the firm's essential business and promote a strong company culture.

Figure 1.2 portrays a project-oriented organisation.

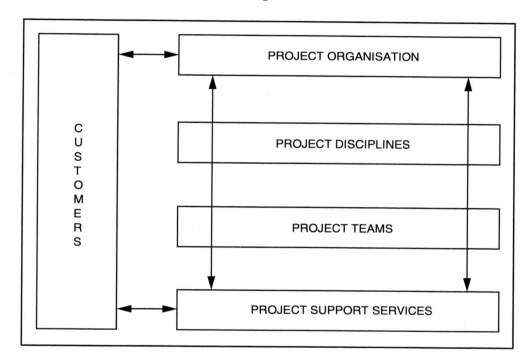

Figure 1.2 Example of a project organisation

Project-oriented organisations are characterised by:

*   Little or no division of labour.

*   Strong emphasis placed on staff competency-based skills, such as: analytical reasoning, delegation, influencing, initiative and leadership.

*   High performance management systems.

*   Project led rather than product led.

*   Few vertical boundaries.

*   Open communications policy.

*   Strong change management culture.

*   No blame culture.

*   Empowered staff.

Underpinning project organisations are:

- Strong project managers, with superior commercial skills.

- Effective project management teams.

- Good project management procedures and practices.

- Rigorous project control methodology.

- Management systems which support the project organisation.

Project Organisations and Projects

Some practitioners of management now consider project organisations to be the shape of things to come. If we subscribe to this view then project management is concerned with managing the entity called 'project'.

There is no single universal definition of a project, although some definitions do have similar structures. Common to many project definitions are:

- projects consume a variety of resources;

- projects have a specific start and end point;

- projects have an owner;

- projects have a specific budget;

- projects have finite objectives.

If we rearrange these five points into a more coherent definition, a project could be defined as:

> 'a unique undertaking with a concise start and end date, a finite budget and resource allocation, and a defined outcome.'

The Scope of This Report

There are four remaining chapters within this report. These chapters are organised as follows:

Chapter 2: Introducing The Project Manager. In this chapter, we discuss the role of the (modern) project manager, and his/her team; how to build teams and team relationships; and which managerial styles are effective in managing projects and project teams.

Chapter 3: Key Requirements For Project Managers. In this chapter, we discuss the key competencies and skills required by modern project managers including hard

skills: project methodologies, planning, risk assessment and financial appraisal. Soft skill sets such as leadership, creativity and motivation are also covered.

Chapter 4: Training And Development. In this chapter, we look at the various options for professional development and ongoing career training, including where to go for such training in order to improve performance and opportunities for future responsibilities of the role.

Chapter 5: Managing Projects. In this final chapter, we outline and define the nature of projects and how the project manager orchestrates the successful delivery of such projects. The importance of whole lifecycle project management, from inception, feasibility, design and implementation to final handover and disposal is discussed in some detail. Project risk is also examined and the sources of risk identified, with advice on how to manage risk and uncertainty. In planning the project the standard tools and techniques available are discussed, including the modernistic PRINCE methodology. Reference to project management software tools and an approach for appraising such software products is illustrated.

The design stage within the project lifecycle can present the project manager with a number of problems at the technical and organisational level. These issues are highlighted and discussed within the project management framework. Finally, the implementation and handover phases represent significant challenges to a project manager. Effective implementation and handover requires the integration and co-ordination of specialist skills. One of the main barriers to successful completion of the project is conflict. How to identify and manage conflict within the project lifecycle is covered and a model is presented to help identify those barriers which prevent successful implementation of the project.

2 Introducing the project manager

The project manager is an integral part of the project organisation and provides the (underpinning) knowledge which is required to sustain performance and increase company profits.

Defining the Project Manager

There are many definitions of what a project manager is and does, for example 'a *person with overall responsibility for completing the project successfully*'. This definition, however, sells the project manager short; the following definition, developed by the author through brainstorming, is perhaps more representative:

> 'A **Project Manager** is concerned with creating wealth through the optimisation and management of all organisational resources.'

The role and authority of a project manager can vary from executive responsibility in a line management sense to that of a manager by persuasion. His span of control over personnel, budgets and assets will also vary from project to project.

The Project Manager's Job Role

One may identify 14 generic elements of any job role. I have used these to demonstrate the job profile for a project manager in Table 2.1.

Table 2.1 Project manager: basic job elements

1. Task	Manage project resources
2. Method	Directing and controlling
3. Technology	Computer software project tools
4. Variety	Moderate – high
5. Sequencing	Substantial latitude
6. Timing	Open (project dependent)
7. Pace	Self-determined
8. Quality	Usually predetermined (e.g. BS 5750)
9. Specialisation	Moderate – low
10. Interdependence	High
11. Partialness	Whole project
12. Performance	To time and within budget
13. Monitoring	Project board
14. Accountability	Project board interviews

Source: adapted from Dawson (1988)

Leadership and the Project Manager

You will by now have gathered that project managers play a vital role in adding value to organisations. Delivering value-added projects requires all project managers to adopt the role of leader, coach and mentor.

Despite the increased use of project management methodologies, lack of leadership and internal conflict are cited as the principal reasons why many project managers fail to achieve their objectives.

Prime Factors Leading to Project Failure

- Lack of leadership related to:
  – poor human skills,
  – poor technical skills,
  – lack of influencing skills,
  – lack of authority.

- Failure to specify project goals and targets.

- Poor planning and project estimating.

- Inadequate project management methods.

- Lack of understanding of project management methodologies.

- Lack of team participation in problem-solving.

- Lack of team spirit and sense of mission within project team.

John Adaire (1990), writing in the book *Understanding Motivation*, identified six functions associated with leadership:

1. **Planning:** seeking available information; defining group tasks or goals; making a workable plan.

2. **Initiating:** briefing the group, allocating tasks; setting group standards.

3. **Controlling:** maintaining group standards; ensuring progress towards objects; prodding actions and decisions.

4. **Supporting:** expressing acceptance of individual contributions; encouraging and disciplining; creating team spirit; relieving tension with humour; reconciling disagreements.

5. **Informing:** clarifying task and plan; keeping the group informed; receiving information from the group; summarising ideas and suggestions.

6. **Evaluating:** checking feasibility of ideas; testing consequence; evaluating group performance, helping the group to evaluate itself.

As a project manager (and leader) you are responsible for motivating, directing, assigning tasks, assessing performance, inspiring by example, coaching and following up. With respect to leadership, project managers have two main functions. These are:

1.   Getting the job done, and

2.   Developing good relationships.

Getting the Job Done

To accomplish the job, the project manager should ensure that his/her *team* and each individual in it knows:

- what their role is;

- how they are going to be assessed (measures of performance etc.);

- their authority to make decisions;

- the degree of management that will be exercised over them;

- the rewards and discipline that will be used.

Definition of a Project Team

A project team may be defined as:

> 'a group of individuals working together for the benefit of the project and the whole organisation.'

The fundamental strength of the project team is focus: everything the individual team members do should be concentrated on making the project successful. Project teams (with the right leader) can excel at quick, efficient delivery.

Team Building

To be an effective project manager you must demonstrate to your project team that:

- you know where you want to go;

- you know how they are going to get there;

- you know what is expected of each team member;

- you know what you are doing;

- you know their strengths and weaknesses, can capitalise on the former and help overcome the latter.

Developing Good Relationships

Antoine de Saint-Exupery is credited with saying: 'There is no joy except in human relationships.' To develop good relationships the project manager should:

- Find time to listen to the individual team members (see Table 2.2): leaders cannot lead if they are out of touch with the feelings of the group.

- Pay attention to the individual's needs, in particular their need to feel a sense of personal achievement in their roles. Give recognition for achievements, to feel that the job itself is challenging, and to know that they are advancing in experience and knowledge.

- Treat group members as equals, without loosing the capacity to exert authority when necessary; remember, we tend to perform at about the same level as those people who are close to us.

Table 2.2 Characteristics of a good listener

- Maintains eye contact during conversation
- Communicates verbally
- Uses body language
- Appears attentive, alert, interested and involved
- Encourages talking through use of questions
- Listens to comprehend
- Does not command the conversation

Team Relationships

Project managers tend to have two types of immediate players:

1. Those who are there because of their formal position (e.g. task managers).

2. Those who are there because of their *personal relationship* with the project manager. This latter group is sometimes referred to as the project manager's inner circle.

Given the complexity of some projects, project managers need allies: people who will support the project when the going gets tough. The project manager's inner circle can be crucial in such circumstances. In contrast to task managers, the inner circle is usually made up of managers of similar rank – they are managers with pull and authority. They will also have influence over resources (cash, people, assets, etc.) within the organisation.

Such managers have responsibilities (to the project) beyond their usual functional designations. Such responsibilities may include:

- Ensuring functional expertise on the project.

- Representing the functional perspective on the project.

- Ensuring that functionally dependent objectives are met.

- Ensuring that functional issues impacting on the team are raised pro-actively within the team.

Project Charter

Project teams and supporting managers need to have a clear and concise mission statement. One way to capture the mission is in an explicit, measurable *project charter* which sets out the broad performance objectives. Such mission statements are normally drawn up prior to starting the project. Personnel joining the project team are expected to share and own the charter. Remember: the charter statement should be representative of what the team is setting out to achieve.

The following project charter was written by a project director working for a major oil company in the North Sea, and demonstrates the principle of what a charter should encompass.

Example of Project Charter Statement

'It is the mission of the Liverpool Bay Development Project to provide the facilities for the production and transportation of oil and gas reserves in Douglas, Hamilton, Hamilton North and Lennox fields in a manner which **adds the greatest value** to Hamilton Oil Company Limited and our partner companies.

This will be accomplished by seeking at all times **the most cost-effective solutions,** whether technical, managerial or commercial whilst complying fully with the corporate policy on Health, Safety and Environment.'

Copyright: Hamilton Oil Company Limited, 1994

Project Manager and Managerial Styles

The project manager must be capable of earning the personal respect and commitment of his/her team. Here, personality and management style are clearly very important. Management style has little to do with competence or knowledge but is more entrenched in the individual personality of the project manager.

In my experience, project managers tend to adopt one of the following managerial styles:

- Autocratic – the repressive approach.

- Democratic – the participative approach.

The Autocratic Management Style

This approach is characterised by a reliance on authority–obedience relationships to get work done and the rigid adherence to defined lines of command (as suggested in functional structures) and centralised decision–making. Project managers who adopt this style of management usually find that their team begin to undermine them as morale drops. Project managers should be aware of the effects upon their team if using this style of management.

Several indicators can point to low morale; the most common are:

- Low productivity;
- Poor quality work;
- High staff turnover;
- Negative rumours (or criticism);
- General insubordination.

The Democratic Management Style

An alternative approach to the autocratic style of management is the democratic style. This participative style of management is characterised by the sharing of responsibility and reliance on team members' own willingness to take whatever actions are required of them without resulting in punishment. As a project manager you will be expected to use positive incentives to invigorate staff to improve their work rate or reward them for notable performance.

The project manager who adopts this democratic style will have an increased chance of successfully completing the project. Establishing a positive *esprit de corps* within the project team gives the project manager a sense of well-being, trust and morale.

Characteristics of Team Morale

Characteristics of morale include:

- good internal communication within the group;
- no blame culture;
- high sense of loyalty;
- clear sense of job purpose;
- clear leadership;
- high quality work;
- positive sense of ownership.

This is only a sample of the characteristics of high morale; however, it does represent a barometer for a high performance project team.

3 Key requirements for project managers

As suggested in Chapter 1, project managers were once in a minority; today, however, the professional project manager is a sought-after commodity. People who become project managers tend to display similar characteristics; in the main they tend to be competitive, quick-thinking, hard-driving and ambitious individuals who know their own mind and are pro-active managers. In essence, pro-active means the ability to shape the future, to make things happen.

Key Competencies of the Job

Two of the key competencies a project manager must possess are self-assurance and the ability to influence. A study carried out by Thamhain and Wilemon (1977), *Leadership, Conflict, and Program Management Effectiveness,* identified nine areas of influence available to project managers. They are:

1. **Authority:** the legitimate hierarchical right to issue orders.

2. **Assignment:** the project manager's perceived ability to influence work assignments.

3. **Budget:** the project manager's perceived ability to authorise others' use of discretionary funds.

4. **Promotion:** the project manager's perceived ability to improve a worker's position.

5. **Money:** the project manager's perceived ability to increase a worker's monetary remuneration.

6. **Penalty:** the project manager's perceived ability to dispense or cause punishment.

7. **Work challenge:** an intrinsic motivational factor capitalising on a worker's enjoyment of doing a particular task.

8. **Expertise:** special knowledge the project manager possesses and others deem important.

9. **Friendship:** friendly, personal relationships between the project manager and others.

As a project manager you will face situations where these nine influences will be invaluable to you, especially when dealing with conflict or disagreement between managers or team members. In addition, professional project managers need to build up a repertoire of competencies if they are to become effective doers.

The UK Association of Project Managers have identified 40 key competencies that project managers should possess. These competencies are listed in Appendix A.

Suggested Key Competencies for Project Managers

Based on my own experience as a practising professional project manager, the minimum repertoire of competencies needed by project managers today are listed in Table 3.1. Although not exhaustive they represent, in my opinion, the key competencies for the job.

Table 3.1 Key competencies for project managers

1. **Analytical:** must be able to examine information and extract details for making decisions.

2. **Awareness:** must be able to understand the broader implications of decisions made and how they affect other members of the project team.

3. **Change oriented:** should demonstrate a desire to initiate and contribute to the implementation of change in services and systems, and the ability to maintain effectiveness in changing environments.

4. **Cost conscious:** must maintain a responsible attitude towards making decisions within the scope of the project role.

5. **Customer awareness:** must consider the implications for the customer (internal and external) in all business decisions and show awareness of customer needs and the importance of meeting agreed customer requirements.

6. **Delegation:** must be able to allocate decision-making and task responsibility to appropriate team members, using skills and potential effectively.

7. **Detail conscious:** must accomplish tasks through showing concern for all aspects of the job, ensuring precision and accuracy.

8. **Diplomatic:** must be able to evaluate a situation and decide on the best course of action to take to gain willing cooperation and avoid conflict.

9. **Explorative thinking:** must be able to challenge assumptions and to solve problems by different methods.

10. **Interpersonal skills:** must be able to relate to staff and customers at all levels in a confident manner.

11. **Leadership:** must be pro-active, keep staff informed and understand the importance of leading by example; must be prepared to take responsibility for his/her decisions.

12. **Negotiating:** must be able to successfully reach an agreement by discussion.

13. **Oral communication:** must be able to convey information and instructions that can be understood.

14. **Team work:** must be able to maintain good relationships with colleagues, work as part of a team and follow instructions.

Source: Competencies (1–14), London Underground Limited, 1993.

Key Skills of the Job

The primary difference between a competency and a skill is that a skill will be made up from a number of competencies. Project managers are not normally selected for their competencies alone; they must possess a range of hard and soft skill sets if they are to be successful managers.

Hard Skills

Project managers come from many disparate backgrounds and often bring to the job a range of technical skills. Whilst there is a cross disciplinary framework within project management, the body of knowledge is nevertheless continually changing. Project managers can draw upon a great range of skill sets from areas such as information technology, construction and engineering. The hard skills normally associated with project management are listed in Table 3.2 and are discussed further in Chapter 5.

Table 3.2 Project manager's required hard skills set

1.	Project methodologies (such as PRINCE)
2.	Planning (as in PERT, CPM and Gantt techniques)
3.	Risk assessment
4.	Financial appraisal (as in NPV and IRR techniques)
5.	Quality assurance
6.	Quantitative (as in statistical techniques)
7.	Programmes management
8.	Configuration management
9.	Data models and software related products
10.	Project management software products

Terms used above:
PRINCE: PRojects IN a Controlled Environment.
PERT: Program Evaluation Review Technique.
CPM: Critical Path Method.
NPV: Net Present Value.
IRR: Internal Rate of Return.
Gantt: A planning chart. Activities are listed in vertical sequence and their durations portrayed horizontally on an appropriate timescale.

Soft Skills

If you are to prosper as a project manager you will need to master a range of soft skills; soft skills are important pathways to delivering successful projects. Unlike

hard skills, soft skills can take years of experience before you become proficient in their use (see Table 3.3).

Some of the soft skills identified in Table 3.3 are obviously more valuable than others; however, knowing which soft skills to master is, regrettably (for many), an arbitrary choice.

Table 3.3 Suggested soft skills set for project managers

1.	Communication skills
2.	Creativity skills
3.	Interacting (social) skills
4.	Judgement skills
5.	Leadership skills
6.	Listening skills
7.	Motivation skills
8.	Political skills
9.	Presentation skills
10.	Time Management skills

Many of the skills we develop in our early years, such as listening and verbal and non-verbal communication are invaluable assets to the project manager. For instance, knowing how to read and assess situations within the project environment, and interacting with peers and other managers are all essential skills.

According to de Bono (1991), writing in *I Am Right You Are Wrong*, language is probably the single most important barrier to progress. He states: 'It is possible that we simply cannot progress any further because we have come up against the ultimate limit of language.'

All managers (project or otherwise) communicate their ideas, thoughts and actions through the media of language: verbal dialogue and the written word. In my experience, too many project managers fail to sell their ideas (and influence outcomes) because of their deficiency in the use of the English language or the written word.

In my business, Information Technology professionals are not well known for their ability to communicate with their clients. The following extract from a factual report would make many non-information technology managers scream in mental pain.

Subject: Customer Management Strategy:

Please could you give me your comments on the attached document as soon as possible. Note that the product configuration baseline adds explicit performance limits to the sub-system compatibility testing, thus a large portion of the interface, co-ordination and communication requires considerable systems analysis and trade-off studies to arrive at any discreet configuration mode, e.g. a constant flow of effective information adds over-riding performance constraints to the structured design based on systems engineering concepts.

Source: Barry Sterndale Bennett, Visiting Lecturer; University of Westminster, 1993.

Project Manager's Communications Checklist

The following checklist (Table 3.4) may prove useful when communicating with others – whether managers, peers, subordinates or other external parties.

Table 3.4 Project manager's communications checklist

- Keep your objectives in mind.

- Establish a pattern of communication which can be followed.

- Use plain language (don't make it complex).

- Allow thinking time for responses to questions.

- Analyse responses (i.e. what does the respondent seem to be saying to me?).

- When writing reports etc., keep your readership in mind at all times. Learn to recognise the difference between factual, instructional and leading reports.

  - *Factual report:* a straightforward statement of the facts to give people an accurate record, for example a feasibility report on a new computer system.

  - *Instructuctional report:* a step-by-step description to tell people about new procedures, for example a functional requirements specification for a new computer system.

  - *Leading report:* this report is known as such because you are leading the reader towards a decision – the one you want him/her to make, for example the purchase of a new computer system to manage maintenance operations.

- Don't *overestimate* your reader's, knowledge and blind them with science, or *underestimate* it and bore them to tears.

- Remember, however good your ideas, they may get rejected if you fail to take account of your audience's special interests, likes and dislikes. The truth has many faces, and it is only sensible to feature the one most likely to appeal to him/her.

4   Training and development

You will have gathered from Chapter 3 that project management embraces a wide variety of competencies and skills. Acquiring such competencies and skills requires the individual project manager to take ownership and responsibility for his/her own career development.

In planning your career development it is advisable to draw up a career plan. A career plan is (normally) composed of three components, namely:

1.   **Education and training:** this is concerned with the formal development of the knowledge and skills required to carry out the duties and responsibilities of the job.

2.   **Internal job development:** this is concerned with building on the skills already acquired in order to improve performance and provide opportunities for individual growth.

3.   **Career development:** this concerns future career prospects and opportunities (and in part succession planning) within or outside the organisation.

Education and Training

Education and training to acquire knowledge and skills can be gained through both formal and informal means (Figure 4.1).

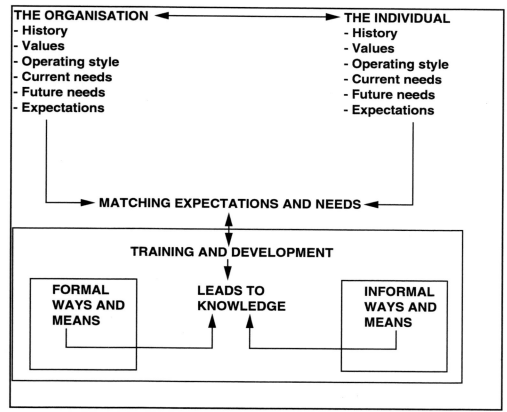

Figure 4.1 Model for knowledge-based training

Although the mechanisms are different, the aims, however, are the same:

- to increase the chance of success in the job,

- to shorten learning time so that the required level of competence can be attained as soon as possible,

- to improve on-the-job performance,

- to build upon and extend the range of skills,

- to help the individual develop their capabilities.

Formal and Informal Training (how and where to get it)

Project managers can acquire the formal knowledge and skills they need in a number of different ways: for example, by attending training courses which lead to a recognised competency-based qualification such as a National Vocational Qualification (NVQ), or by attendance (full or part time) at an institution of learning, e.g. a college or university. In fact, many large and medium sized enterprises are now increasingly recruiting project managers direct from college or university.

Research would suggest that project management is embracing a wide spectrum of managerial, legal and behavioural disciplines. Some UK universities and higher education establishments now offer Diploma, MSc or MBA degrees in project management (see Appendix B). The modules offered, which obviously vary, cover project principles, project planning, project finance and project practice.

Such courses aim to fill gaps in the project manager's knowledge by increasing their understanding and skills. Many of the courses listed in Appendix B offer a broad perspective; for example, some courses have a general management focus, where project management students learn from other professional occupations and study subjects such as: economics, accounting, strategy, information systems, organisational behaviour, contract law, and resource planning. Although many of the subjects covered fall into the hard skills set, there are many programmes which incorporate a high degree of soft skills such as leadership, teamwork, presentation and negotiating skills.

Candidates wishing to undertake an MSc or MBA programme must usually possess a good first degree or be a member of a relevant professional body, and have between two and five years professional experience.

For those people not wanting to undertake a formal academic course there is an alternative. In 1992 the UK Association of Project Managers launched a certification scheme with the aim of increasing the professional standing of project managers. The programme is broadly divided into four skill categories. These are:

1.   Project management,

2.   Organisation and people,

3.   Processes and procedures, and

4.   General management.

According to the Association's literature, certification is aimed at assessing an individual's competence in managing projects. Competence is defined by the APM as: 'the ability to acquire and apply knowledge and skills in the appropriate context.'

The APM also offers training in individual skill sets e.g. team building, scheduling, estimating, law, industrial relations and information technology. Unlike the MSc and MBA, the APM's certification scheme is a test of competence and not one of academic achievement. Consequently there is no academic hurdle to overcome: each level is individually assessed by a panel of professional assessors.

If you are unable to attend a formal college, university or professional institution, you might consider attending seminars or talks within your own organisation. Although perhaps not as stimulating or interactive, they are no less a useful alternative.

Evaluating Your Commitment and Suitability

It is perhaps worth pointing out that project managers embarking on a course of professional training will need more then ability. In essence you will need:

- A high degree of commitment and motivation.

- A sense of purpose for learning.

- A willingness to participate and share information and experiences.

- A sense of humour (for when the going gets tough – which it will from time to time).

Internal Job Development

Training which is not supplemented by continued professional development will in the long term have little intrinsic value to both the individual and the organisation. People will learn and retain more knowledge if their formal/informal education is supplemented by ongoing on-the-job training and development.

Ongoing job development can take many forms, including structured appraisals, mentoring and coaching. Coaching (unlike structured appraisals and mentoring) is a personal, on-the-job method designed to develop individual skills. It broadly consists of:

- making staff think through how they are coping with the job;

- identifying strengths and weaknesses of the individual, building on the strengths and working towards eliminating the weaknesses;

- using situations as they occur as teaching opportunities;

- spending time with the individual looking at specific management issues and how these relate to the job in question.

With the right person, coaching is a cost-effective method of developing the skills and competencies of project management staff. The coach should ensure that feedback is plentiful, accurate, to the point and timely. The coach should also ensure that the person concerned can apply what knowledge has been learned quickly and with long-term benefit, i.e. not simply acquire a skill that may be used just for a few days and then discarded. This is an important point and is worth stressing. It is my experience that many potential project managers are not aware of the long-term benefits of skill retention. Some adopt the attitude: 'What's the point of retaining all this stuff, if I'm only going to put it into practice once in a blue moon?'

Sometimes they are (of course) right, but usually they are too 'green' and don't understand that what they are learning will eventually be important. If you are a student of project management, don't be myopic. Think ahead – the better you understand the demands of the job, the more you will understand why practical on-the-job learning is important.

Career Development

Planning your career and life portfolio is the essence of your future. In planning your career, there are three fundamental questions you need to ask yourself:

1.   Where am I now?   (e.g. assistant project manager)

2.   Where do I want to be?   (e.g. a project director)

3.   How do I get there?   (e.g. what goals do I set myself)

Answering questions 1 and 2 are easy; question 3 is perhaps a bit more difficult and requires you to take stock of your own situation and to question all aspects of your working life. For example:

- How did I decide that I wanted a career in project management?

- How did I get where I am today?

- How satisfied am I with my current position?

- What type of relationships do I have with work colleagues?

- What is my attitude to work?

- What are my major life achievements to date?

- What lessons have I learned in the job?

- With respect to the job, what are my strengths and weaknesses?

- What are my most marketable skills (and what are my least)?

- What can I do to advance my present job skills?

- What would I like to see happen in my career over the next ten years?

Future Career Goals

In assessing your future career goals, you must ask yourself what assistance and resources will be needed to achieve them. If, for example, you are a project assistant and your ambition is to become a project director, your goals must be focused to this end. The assets that are going to have the greatest impact are:

1.   your talents, competencies and skills,

2.   your intelligence,

3.   your motivation, and

4.   your friends, superiors and subordinates.

Your future career plan should include:

- an audit of your current organisation's needs;

- an audit of peer competition (make a list of people who you think are now or in the future ready to replace existing managers – look at the qualities of such people);

- an examination of the external market opportunities – what type of person is being recruited;

- what professional and technical knowledge will you require to fulfil your ambition(s).

Career Goal Action Plans

Finally, for each of your future career goals:

- determine how you will benefit from accomplishing your goals.

- identify the obstacles you will have to overcome.

- clarify the skills and knowledge you will need to develop.

- identify the people whose cooperation and help you will need.

- note the short-term objectives you need to achieve in order to accomplish your goals.

Check that you can apply the following criteria to each of your goals:

Specific:	have I been specific enough?
Challenging:	will they stretch my skills?
Realistic:	can I realistically achieve them?
Actionable:	can I do something proactive about them?
Measurable:	can I check my progress?

Copyright: Accountancy Personnel, Hays Business Services Group, 1995.

5   Managing projects

In Chapter 2 we discussed the project manager's post and role in delivering and managing projects. In this chapter we outline and define the nature of projects (whole lifecycle) and how the project manager orchestrates the successful delivery of such projects.

The Project Lifecycle

It is perhaps convenient to think about projects as going through a pre-defined lifecycle within a managed framework. The Association of Project Managers defines the Project Lifecycle as: 'a sequence of phases through which a project must pass.'

A review of the project management literature suggests that the type of lifecycle methodology used, together with the respective control systems, are crucial to delivering value added projects. A typical project lifecycle is comprised of three stages: (1) birth, (2) life, and (3) death. Table 5.1 shows three lifecycle methodologies which reflect the different approaches and practices adopted by industry-specific organisations.

Although industry-specific lifecycle methodologies are widely adopted, the generally accepted sequence is shown in Table 5.2. In practice, the stages frequently overlap and sometimes the boundaries between them can become indistinct; it is, however, essential that the project manager maintains involvement throughout all stages.

Table 5.1 Types of lifecycle methodologies

Construction	Manufacturing	I.T. (Information Technology)
Inception	Customer Needs	Concept
Feasibility Study	Concept Design	Feasibility
Outline Proposals	Feasibility Study	User Requirements
Scheme Design	Preliminary Design	Functional Design
Detail Design	Final Design	Development
Construction	Prototype	Functionality Test
Occupancy	Market Field Test	Implementation
Renew/Replace	Manufacturing	Post Concept Audit
Demolish	Market Introduction	Operational Use
	Market Follow-up	Support
	Market Withdrawal	Withdraw From Use

Phase One (Birth)

It is important to recognise that project management (and the project manager) will be required at all three stages of the lifecycle. The initial phase (birth) of the project will normally present particular difficulties. For example, the inception, feasibility

and planning stages often require inputs from specialists (such as accountants, marketing people, designers, developers and other types of specialists). As a project manager you must be able to establish credibility and rapport with such people whose input is vital in getting the project established.

Table 5.2 Generic project lifecycle

Birth	Life	Demise
Inception	Implementation	Withdrawal
Feasibility	Handover	Disposal
Plan	Operational use	
Design (detail)	Support	

Inception and Feasibility

Prior to the commencement of a project it is critical to establish that it is going to offer the business value-for-money. It is essential, therefore, to evaluate the project requirements with regard to the organisation's business goals. For example:

- How will investing in the project further the competitiveness of the business or organisation?

- What has led to the demand for the project?

- What is the payback period of the project investment?

- What are the project timescales?

- What resources will be needed (i.e. people, plant, materials and capital)?

- What are the main functional requirements of the project and/or its constituent parts?

Project Inception

Projects occur as a result of one or more of a whole range of influences, pressures and demands on, or within, an organisation. For example, in the transport industry such influences range from health and safety requirements to the need to accommodate new civil engineering works and information systems as a result of changes in infrastructure requirements, processes and technology.

At the inception stage of a project it is normal practice to set up a *Steering Committee* and invite those people who have (or will have) a stake in the project. Such stakeholders will include:

- project chairman: normally a senior manager who makes decisions and arbitrates when resolutions are required;

- project sponsor: the person responsible for funding the project;

- project client: the person representing the customer;

- programmes manager: the person responsible for allocating resources to the project;

- project manager: the person responsible for managing and delivering the project.

Why is a Steering Committee needed? The prime purpose of the Steering Committee is to establish the scope of the project by specifying:

- what is to be done (i.e. the project deliverables);

- when it is to be done; and

- at what cost.

Project Feasibility

Prior to authorising any investment capital the Steering Committee will want to establish that the project is going to yield positive savings/benefits for the company. To establish this a feasibility study is normally undertaken. The feasibility study is a detailed investigation of the project requirements, costs, risks and tangible benefits, and involves:

- deciding the scope and objectives of the project;
- determining the project requirements;
- evaluating solutions
- planning an implementation strategy; and
- preparing a cost/benefit analysis.

The feasibility study should also provide and seek to deliver:

1.   a profitable outcome for the organisation (i.e. a positive Net Present Value or NPV*);

2.   what the customer wants;

3.   a rewarding and learning experience for all those who (will) take part in the project.

Evaluating Project Risk

Risk analysis consists of two processes: the identification of risk factors, and the assessment of their effect on the project. Risk represents the main reason why many

---

* The term NPV is a yardstick for the assessment of a project based on discounted cash flow techniques. A zero NPV indicates that the project repays the capital invested plus the minimum accepted return. A positive NPV indicates a better return, while a negative NPV indicates a worse return. See J. McManus, A practical approach to project appraisal, *Management Accounting*, November 1981.

projects fail to get beyond the feasibility stage. When undertaking the feasibility study it is important to identify the sources of risk (Table 5.3). A wide field of literature exists on risk analysis, tools and techniques, ranging from computer models to basic statistical representations such as probability analysis. The treatment of risk can be as complex as you want to make it (Figure 5.1).

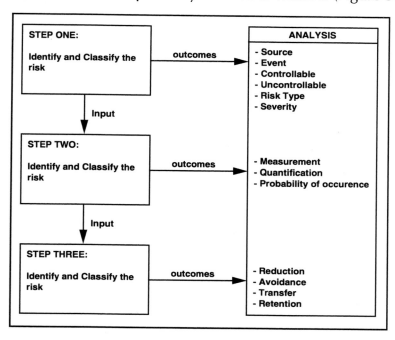

Figure 5.1 The risk assessment process

Ultimately, however, all risk can be classified into one or more of the following:

*   political: e.g. legislation, safety and the environment;
*   financial: e.g. cost of capital (interest rates) and inflation;
*   technical: e.g. required technical standards and quality;
*   logistical: e.g. availability of specialist plant or materials;
*   contractual: e.g. ability to see the project through.

Table 5.3 Project vs. associated risk

Typical Project	Source of Risk
Infrastructure or construction	Risks due to weak planning, human errors or 'acts of God'.
New technology or product Research and Development	Risks due to the investment in some new technology or commercial product.
New Military System(s) (e.g. The 'Star Wars' Defense System)	Risks due to hidden political agenda(s), and integrating new technologies for the first time and perhaps due to the wrong trade-off decisions.
New technology development	Risks in unknown technologies, specialist skills and capital investment requirements.

Projects such as the construction of the Channel Tunnel represent significant risk to government and investors alike. High-risk projects such as this are characterised by substantial fixed capital expenditure.

Investors require high rates of return for higher levels of risk. Organisations undertaking high-risk investment projects must seek to achieve higher returns than their shareholders can earn for that level of risk in the capital markets. There is clearly no sense in spending substantial capital unless the benefits predicted (return on investment capital) – and hopefully realised – outweigh the likely expenditure. For example, during the construction phase of the Channel Tunnel the French co-chairman, André Benard, was reported to say:

> 'Eurotunnel is a project which carries risks. We have put certain risks behind us, but there are others of a commercial nature which remain. It is for investors to make their own judgements.'

On 26 May 1994, the *London Evening Standard* newspaper wrote:

> 'The project has ended up costing close on £11 billion after starting off at less than £5 billion. The awkward fact is that £5 billion is probably what the project is worth. One can almost hear the sound of financiers running for cover.'

The formalised structure described in Figure 5.1 is one practical approach to risk assessment (which I have used on many occasions). This approach has the following advantages:

- It enables the financial and technical risk analysis to be undertaken within a controlled framework.

- It forms the basis of the required outcomes from the risk process, namely the transfer of risk into any contractual arrangements.

- It provides an audit trail for the judgements and decisions which were made.

The key to controlling project risk is to identify them from the outset and review the sources continuously throughout the project lifecycle in a systematic manner. Risks should be defined and managed like all other project parameters. The project manager must ask the following questions:

- Who is best positioned to control risk?

- Who can best assimilate the impact of risk?

- Is the customer willing to accept the cost of risk?

- Is the transfer of risk cost-effective?

Planning the Project

Projects which make it through the feasibility stage generally receive the green light to proceed. It is at this point in the cycle that the project manager accepts the task of delivering the required products. Leadership at this stage (see pages 7–10) will set the standard for the whole project and help avoid costly mistakes and difficulties at the design and implementation stages.

The basic group of tools used in project management has remained the same for over a decade. A review of the literature suggests that there are six principal methodologies in use today. These are:

1.   traditional Programme Evaluation Review Techniques or PERT (and Critical Path Method or CPM) methods;

2.   outlining methods;

3.   multi-stage, multi-level, hierarchical planning;

4.   cost and time resource methods;

5.   cost/schedule control systems;

6.   Projects in a Controlled Environment or PRINCE (the UK Government's standard for its computer-based information systems projects).

Methods of planning and control such as PERT, CPM or Gantt charts (Table 3.2, page 14) are used in almost all projects. Indeed, all the above methods display many common characteristics with each other. In planning the project, the project manager must consider how the mix of physical and human resources will be used. And how he/she and his/her team will manage the constraints (time, cost, quality and performance). The planning cycle illustrated in Figure 5.2 outlines the steps to follow in planning the project. The rules the project manager and his/her team should follow are:

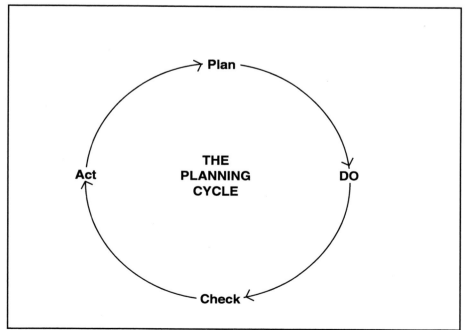

Figure 5.2 The planning cycle

- Plan as much as you can do.

- Do as much as you can check.

- Check as much as you can act upon.

- Act in accordance with the planned objectives and deliverables.

PRINCE (as a planning methodology)

Unlike methods 1–5, the PRINCE (PRojects IN a Controlled Environment) project management methodology provides an intrinsic framework for the project manager in which to plan the project. The UK government organisation, the Central Computer and Telecommunications Agency (CCTA), who market PRINCE, describe the structure of PRINCE plans as:

> 'A commitment to meet identified targets in terms of products, time scales, costs, and quality. Planning is the process of estimating, collecting, sequencing, scheduling and assigning the project's resources to deliver the desired products.'

Within PRINCE a project is subdivided into stages, to provide regular, formal assessment points for senior management to monitor and control the progress of the project.

The standard components of PRINCE are: Organisation, Plans, Controls, Products and Activities.

PRINCE Project Plans

Several plans are required for setting up and controlling a PRINCE (managed) project. These are outlined in Table 5.4.

Table 5.4 PRINCE planning hierarchy

Level/Type of Plan	Produced	Recipient
1. Project resource plan	Post feasibility	Project board members
2. Project technical plan	Post feasibility	Project board members
3. Stage resource plan	End of previous stage	Stage manager
4. Stage technical plan	End of previous stage	Stage manager
5. Exception plan	When necessary	All
6. Detailed resource plan	Any stage as needed	Stage teams
7. Detailed technical plan	Any stage as needed	Stage teams
8. Individual work plan	Any stage as needed	Individual

Source: adapted from the PRINCE manual, Crown copyright, 1990.

Within PRINCE, the size of a given project will determine the number of planning levels and the amount of detail required. When developing these plans, the project manager must:

1.   Identify all the products* to be produced, and define their content and form.

2.   Identify the appropriate quality, methods and performance standards to be used.

3.   Identify the dependencies between products and resources.

4.   Specify the logical sequence of activities based on the identified dependencies.

5.   Estimate and allocate the resources needed to deliver products.

6.   Define timescales and delivery schedules.

7.   Set objectives and allocate responsibilities.

8.   Monitor the plans and facilitate communication.

PRINCE is increasingly being used within the private and public sectors. Given this situation project managers should develop formal skills in the use of the methodology.

Work Breakdown Structure (WBS)

As a basis for scheduling, budgeting and resource allocation, large projects should be broken down into small packages of work. One method of achieving this is the work breakdown structure (WBS). A key element within PRINCE the WBS is:

> A product oriented hierarchical breakdown of the product into its constituent end items (or parts) and then into the principal activities needed to produce these.

It could be reasoned that the primary function of the WBS is that of an accounting tool for summing up the costs of tasks related to all activities. From the project sponsor's perspective, the WBS has a significance in that it helps him/her understand (and keep track) of how the cash is being spent.

The published work plan should be structured in accordance with the WBS. Like all project plans, the WBS is likely to go through several changes throughout the project lifecycle. Such changes usually result from trade-off decisions in managing the project constraints.

Project Management Software Tools

Given the complexity of planning projects under conditions of uncertainty, many organisations now use project management computer software tools. There are several hundred products available on the market. The market for such products can be broken down into three levels:

---

*The term 'Product' in PRINCE refers to any output from a project. PRINCE distinguishes between management products (which are produced as part of the management of the project), technical products (which are those products which make up the system) and quality products (which are produced for or by the quality process).

1.   Basic scheduling packages (which contain no logic).

2.   Moderately integrated systems which contain some basic logic to enable resource planning to take place.

3.   Sophisticated systems which offer multi-level modules, true integration between resource planning, scheduling, costing, financial planning, contract management and 'what if' scenario planning.

The cost of such software tools can range from a few hundred pounds for PC products to tens of thousands of pounds for mainframe products. Although the method(s) of appraising such products are beyond the scope of this report, it is perhaps worth illustrating the basic approach to selection:

1.   Establish (and agree) a budget.

2.   Draw up a User Requirements Specification (URS).

3.   Identify key attributes within the URS.

4.   Review the market and select those packages which closely match the URS.

5.   Undertake site visits (if appropriate) to see the product(s) in operation.

6.   Select the desired package.

7.   Draw-up training requirements for users.

8.   Implement the package and train all users.

The advantages of using project management software tools are:

•   The ability to undertake 'what if?' scenarios.

•   The ability to make cost planning, cost monitoring and resource forecasting simpler and more effective.

•   The ability to produce resource update reports at will.

•   The ability to filter, and transfer information to groups of people, through the use of Local or Wide Area Computer Networks.

Design (within project management)

One key to successful project implementation (Phase Two) lies in designing the product to meet the expectations of the client(s) or organisation. The design stage can present the project manager with a number of problems: for example, the coordination and control of specialist resources can be particularly difficult, and decisions made during the design stage will usually have a major influence over the final total project cost.

It has been observed by Birchall and Newcomb (1985) that:

> 'Designers often seek to develop a technically advanced solution
> incorporating the latest gadgetry. This may not be in the best interest of
> the client, particularly when the designer insists on late changes so as to
> ensure the latest technology. A late change to effect marginal
> performance improvements may have cost and time penalties which far
> exceed the long-term benefits derived, but which at the time of the
> change were not fully appreciated.'

The Design Process

The design process can be considered as passing through a number of phases
which the project manager must be aware of. Professor Joe Black, formally of Bath
University, described this process as the 'seven C's' of successful design, namely:
Customer, Competition, Costs, Concept, Compromise, Construction and
Communication.

My own 'version' of Professor Black's 7 Cs is outlined in Table 5.5.

Table 5.5 The 7 Cs design process

1.	Customer: Origin of requirement, need to meet the customer's requirement, fit for purpose.
2.	Competition: Common issues relevant to the management of design. Vested interests, patents, trade marks, intellectual property rights.
3.	Cost: How much will it cost to make, will it meet the economic objectives of the business?
4.	Concept: Solution to the basic problem:
	– operational and environmental aspects,
	– design specifications,
	– principles of the system,
	– requirements of system features with schemes.
5.	Compromise: How will the product be made?, Who will make it?
6.	Construction: Detail specification, prototype, test, install, use, maintain.
7.	Communication: Decisions, client changes, agreement to prototype specifications, management control.

Source: adapted from Professor J. Black, Bath University.

Hollins Design Methodology

Dr Bill Hollins (of the Management Centre, University of Westminster, London), a
leading authority in design, has developed a methodology and framework for total
design. Hollins' methodology endeavours to assist design teams increase their
awareness of poor design by focusing attention on the design mix.

The methodology was based on research undertaken by Stuart Pugh in the early 1980s. Pugh's research led to the Design Core to assist designers in developing cost-effective design specifications. The term Design Core is used to define a conceptual framework – sometimes referred to as a design model.

According to Hollins 'not all elements in the Design Core carry equal weight.' The important elements depend partly on the particular product or service under design. Those identified generically by Hollins include: reliability, safety, aesthetics, maintainability, ergonomics and price.

Hollins' robust and proven model consists of 13 layers and is fully compatible with both the PRINCE and WBS previously discussed.

The Engineering Construction Economic Development Council's *Guidelines for the Management of Major Projects in the Process Industries* provides relevant advice to project managers for managing the design stage of all types of projects. Key points include:

- **Design programme and budget:** all design decisions should be planned in detail taking account of the needs of procurement, manufacturing, construction and commissioning.

- **Design contracts:** contracts need to be designed to create co-operative relationships.

- **Design budget:** the design budget must be realistic and supported by simple and effective communication to all project participants.

- **Walk the job:** all project managers need to walk the design offices (manufacturing plants and construction sites) to get a feel for what is really happening, to ask questions and to identify and prevent problems.

Phase Two (Life)

This phase of the project lifecycle includes: implementation, handover, operational use and support, and presents a significant intellectual and physical challenge to the project manager. To echo this point, at a key project management leadership conference in Chicago, USA, in June 1995, delegates were told that their mistakes will cost $81 billion (£48 billion) in cancelled projects in 1995, even successful projects will waste $59 billion (£35 billion) in cost and time overruns due to poor implementation and lack of management control.

Implementation

Effective implementation requires the integration and coordination of specialist capabilities. Integration is, in the opinion of most project management professionals, the **key** distinguishing function of the project manager. Integration according to the APM involves: 'bringing people and things together to perform effectively.' Integration is coordination and control. The APM defines effective integration as:

- an effective personality,
- adequate technical knowledge,
- and organisational, managerial and people skills.

One of the main barriers to integration and effective implementation is conflict. As previously discussed (pages 7–10) leadership and conflict are cited as the principal reasons why project managers fail to achieve their objectives. Writing in *Industrial Engineering* in May 1992, Deborah Kezsbom identified 13 conflict categories which impede the successful delivery of projects. From Kezsbom's list I have selected five definitions which, in my opinion, have the greatest impact on the implementation stage.

1. **Managerial and administrative procedures:** disagreements that develop over how the project will be managed, the definition of reporting relationships and responsibilities, interface relationships, project scope, work design, plans of execution, negotiated work agreements with other groups, and procedures for administrative support.

2. **Communication:** disagreements resulting from poor information flow among staff or between senior management and technical staff, including such topics as misunderstanding of project-related goals and the strategic mission of the organisation, and the flow of communication from technical staff to senior management.

3. **Resource allocation:** disagreements resulting from the competition for resources (e.g. personnel, materials, facilities and equipment) among project members or across teams, or from lack of resources or downsizing of organisations.

4. **Personality and interpersonal relationships:** disagreements that focus on interpersonal rather than on technical issues, including conflicts that are ego-centred, personality differences, or caused by prejudice or stereotyping.

5. **Technical opinion:** disagreements that arise, particularly in technology-oriented projects, over technical issues, performance specifications technical trade-offs, and the means to achieve performance.

As a project manager you should make every effort to integrate as early as possible the various groups involved in the implementation process. It is an undisputed fact that reducing conflict leads to increased performance. Conflict in the objectives of performance have to be managed – since these invariably affect the time and cost of the project. The model outlined in Figure 5.3 gives one diagnostic approach to effective performance control.

The model outlined in Figure 5.3 should not only seek to identify the negative aspects of performance that could lead to poor implementation, but also highlight opportunities to improve control, quality and costs and reduce the project lead time.

Managing the Implementation Process

In discussing this process, some distinction must be made for the type of project under implementation. For example, the approach adopted for construction projects is somewhat different to that used for software products. The principal differences are related to size, time span, complexity, technology, type of industry and customers.

In the computer industry the accepted implementation process for new computer systems is as follows:

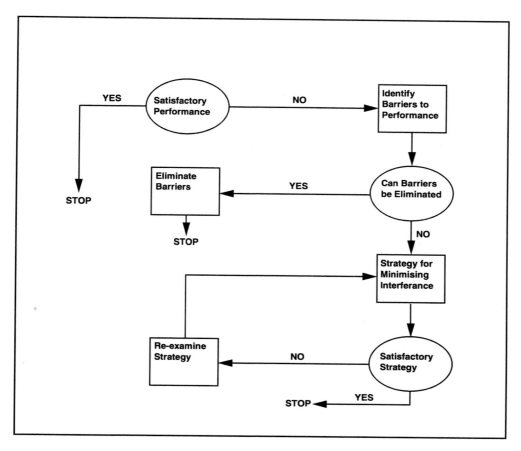

Figure 5.3 A diagnostic model of performance

1.　　　Determine scope and objectives for implementation.

2.　　　Draw up an implementation plan.

3.　　　Deliver training plan.

4.　　　Establish operating environment.

5.　　　Agree service levels.

6.　　　Perform take-on and conversion.

7.　　　Perform system cut-over.

8.　　　Train users.

9.　　　Complete user documentation.

10.　　Perform system handover.

During the implementation phase, the project manager should check:

•　　　that the project plan is monitored and kept up to date;

•　　　that all team members are briefed and know what their roles are within the implementation process (remember to *delegate* – get the persons who will be undertaking the tasks to plan the work: don't feel guilty it's their task, not yours);

•　　　that the cost of implementation is being managed within the agreed budget.

- that any proposed changes are agreed with the project board, recorded and subsequently monitored.

Monitoring the Implementation Process

It is necessary that the actual plan and all comparable costs are monitored throughout the implementation phase, so that comparisons can be made with forecasts and significant differences highlighted. Causes for cost variances include:

- no earned value measures,

- poor organisation and planning,

- poor team communication,

- ill defined objectives,

- lack of budget accountability,

- unforeseen external influences (e.g. market interest rates); and

- poor management.

Monitoring costs is not simply a matter of showing how good the original forecasts were, but should provide an understanding so that subsequent similar projects can benefit from the knowledge gained.

Value of Work Done

Taken in isolation, neither the budget or actual costs are sufficient to show the financial status of a project. What is needed is a way of comparing (and combining) the project cost information to evaluate the Value of Work Done (VOWD). One method of evaluating the VOWD is to use the accounting technique of earned value (or earned value analysis).

Earned value analysis (EVA) was originally used by the US government to monitor large (and complex) defence projects. In order to keep a track of the earned value, many organisations use computer software packages (pages 29-30) for handling the complicated calculations. The advantage of using such packages (in addition to those discussed on pages 29-30) is that they can produce a variety of graphs, indices, variances and forecasts which are based on the three accounting variables:

1.   budget costs;

2.   actual costs;

3.   earned value.

The EVA can be broken down to form a cost breakdown structure (CBS) and then aggregated against the WBS. As the project progresses the actual VOWD can be plotted alongside the forecast values (or the cost of work scheduled). In earned value terms progress is measured as the budgeted VOWD up to a specific calendar date.

Exception Plans

Where changes to the implementation plan are conceivable due to cost or time-scale increases, the project board will more than likely request an exception plan (see Table 5.4, page 28).

Possible reasons for the production of an exception plan are:

- The process of implementing the project is taking longer than was originally envisaged.

- A significant external dependency is not being met, for example a supplier to the project can not deliver on time - due to strike action or closure. To illustrate this point, a small oil-refining company embarked on a project to build a new plant. The company suffered dramatically when it received an unexpected announcement that there would be a three-month interruption in its supply of crude oil; alternative supplies were not as suitable, and caused technical and marketing difficulties:

We were negligent in our approach to our suppliers, in that we did not adequately sustain a relationship with them, to the extent that they did not advise us of their impending refinery closure.

Source: Boddy (1993).

- A major quality or technical deviation cannot be resolved within the defined tolerance, for example the building of new rolling stock for use in metro transit systems.

An exception plan should be comprised of technical, quality and resource plans. The overall plan must describe the cause(s) of the deviation(s), consequences, and the effect on the project as a whole, and must recommend corrective action to the project board.

Handover and Project Closure

On completion of the implementation stage, the project manager will hand over the management and running of the project to its new owners (or users). To achieve this state, the project must be signed off by the owners (and project board) as fit for purpose by matching the agreed specification.

Project Closure

Before closing the project, the project manager and his/her team have an obligation to ensure that all the specified deliverables have been met in accordance with the original specification and that all documentation is in order prior to handover. All such documentation should include any approved specification changes, including any changes which were originally outside the project terms of reference.

The Central Computer and Telecommunications Agency introduction to PRINCE (version 1, E.1, page 4, 3.3 Project Closure) suggests that at the end of a project the

following management activities should take place to ensure that the project is closed in an orderly fashion. They include:

1.   Acceptance letters, which must be prepared and approved.

2.   Project Evaluation Report, which must be prepared and agreed.

3.   Final Report, which must be prepared for the executive committee.

4.   Post-completion Audit, make arrangements for it to be carried out.

Post-Completion Audits

Many projects are subjected to post-completion audits to examine how well they were managed. Projects will be examined to ascertain the significant variances between actual and predicted results against the agreed deliverables. Although sometimes painful they can be useful in pinpointing genuine weak points in the processes and practices used. It is my experience as a practising project manager (researcher and former consultant) that feedback from such post-audits can and do lead to significant improvements and learning.

Phase Three (Demise)

Once implemented, all capital projects have a finite lifespan which, when reached, will render them obsolete. Almost all decisions to withdraw capital items from service are related to five broad considerations:

1.   **Physical obsolescence:** for example, when a building is likely to collapse due to structural failure or when a computer system can no longer be maintained.

2.   **Economic obsolesence:** for example, when the cost to maintain a building, a piece of plant or a computer sytem is more than its replacement cost.

3.   **Functional obsolesence:** for example, when equipment no longer performs the function(s) for which it was built or made.

4.   **Technological obsolesence:** for example, when new high technology products enter the market and make existing technology products redundant.

5.   **Social obsolesence:** for example, when new legislation is passed or introduced which dictates a replacement for reasons other than economic considerations, i.e. when an employeer can no longer guarantee the health and safety of his/her employees.

Withdrawal and Disposal

Withdrawal and disposal of many capital items are now becoming more difficult as companies have to comply with increasing legislation and ecological pressure

groups. Consider the recent difficulties the oil and gas companies have experienced in withdrawing from service platforms in the North Sea. Alternatively, consider the Magnox nuclear power stations which were designed for a life of twenty years, later extended to thirty. According to Hollins and Hollins (1991):

> 'In the design of these stations their **disposal** was barely considered and it is now realised that it will take about a hundred years and cost £800 million to take down each Magnox reactor – and they are still not sure how to do it. Covering them with concrete, painting them green, and calling them a hill was once a serious suggestion.'

The **lesson** is that withdrawal and disposal of capital projects should be considered at the feasibility and design stages (Phase One) (see Table 5.6). Project teams must be educated to consider the ecological and environmental issues around the projects they are involved with. Such levels of public awareness, greater scientific understanding of the interaction between products and the natural environment, and more stringent environmental regulation indicate that a structured framework for disposal is a prerequisite for all capital projects. Such a framework will need to include the following considerations:

*   **Government Agencies:**

    – Government Initiatives
    – Regulations
    – Public Opinion
    – Environmental Issues

*   **Customer Expectations:**
    – Company Policy
    – Financial and Resource Constraints
    – Level of Ability and Knowledge
    – Training Costs

*   **Market Considerations:**
    – Market Considerations (with regard to product lifecycles)
    – Trends and Concerns
    – Opportunities and Threats
    – Market Regulation

Table 5.6 Stages in the disposal of a capital project

1. Approval	Preliminary discussion and agreement on a project disposal strategy.
2. Formulation	Study of various disposal options.
3. Design	Select desired option and design specification.
4. Plans	Formulated plans should be reviewed annually to take into consideration the NPV cost of disposal and the resources needed.
5. Implementing the plan	The date should be annually reviewed to reflect company circumstances

Conclusion

This account of the role of the modern project manager has aimed to present the reader with a balanced view of project management by examining the project organisation and its environment, and the qualities, competencies and skills needed by project managers in order to successfully deliver value added projects under various lifecycle conditions.

In conclusion, as project managers we are living in a rapidly changing world where functional organisations are no longer the cultural norm. The project manager of the 1990s is having to cope with changing structures, work patterns, diminishing resources, conflict and the chameleon-like behaviour of peer managers. To survive in this rapidly changing world the project manager needs an awareness of his/her role and the environment he/she operates in far beyond that of the technical aspects of the job.

Appendix A The Association of Project Managers' list of competencies

Adapted from the APM Certificate Self-Assessment Form

Project Management	Techniques and Procedures
1. Systems Management	22. Work Definition
2. Programme Management	23. Planning
3. Project Management	24. Scheduling
4. Project Lifecycle	25. Estimating
5. Project Environment	26. Cost-Control
6. Project Strategy	27. Performance Measurement
7. Project Appraisal	28. Risk Management
8. Project Success/Failure	29. Value Management
9. Integration	30. Change Control
10. Systems and Procedures	31. Mobilisation
11. Close Out	
12. Post Project Appraisal	
Organisation and People	**General Management**
13. Organisation Design	32. Operations/Technical Management
14. Control and Co-ordination	33. Marketing and Sales
15. Communication	34. Finance
16. Leadership	35. Information Technology
17. Delegation	36. Law
18. Team Building	37. Procurement
19. Conflict Management	38. Quality
20. Negotiation	39. Safety
21. Management Development	40. Industrial Relations

Copyright: Association of Project Managers, 1993.

Appendix B Universities and professional bodies offering project management courses

1.   BRITISH UNIVERSITIES

University of Bradford
Bradford
West Yorkshire
BD7 1DP
Tel: **01274 733466**

Course type: MSc in Development and Project Planning

Brunel The University of West London
Henley Management College
Greenlands
Henley-on-Thames
Oxfordshire
RG9 3AU
Tel: **01491 571454**

Course type: MBA in Project Management

Cranfield University School of Management
Cranfield
Bedfordshire
MK43 0AL
Tel: **01234 751806**

Course type: MSc Degree in Project Management

University of Dundee
Department of Civil Engineering
Dundee
DD1 4HN
Tel: **01382 201604**

Course type: MSc in Construction and Project Management

Imperial College
University of London
Department of Civil Engineering
London
SW7 2BU
Tel: **0171-225 8417**

Course type: Short courses in Project Management

Kingston University
Kingston-upon-Thames
Surrey
Tel: **0181-547 7809**

Course type: Short course programme in Project Management

The University of Reading
Department of Construction Management and Engineering
PO Box 219
Whiteknights
Reading
RG6 2BU
Tel: **01734 318195**

Course type: MSc in Project Management

The Management School
University of Salford
Salford
M5 4WT
Tel: **0161-745 5530**

Course type: Diploma and MSc in Project Management

UMIST
Department of Civil and Structural Engineering
PO Box 88
Manchester
M60 1QD
Tel: **0161-200 4621**

Course type: Diploma and MSc in Engineering Project Management

University of Westminster
School of Architecture and Engineering
35 Marylebone Road
London
NW1 5LS
Tel: **0171-911 5000**

Course type: Short courses in Project Management

2.   PROFESSIONAL BODIES

The Association of Project Managers
85 Oxford Road
High Wycombe
Buckinghamshire
HP11 2DX
Tel: **01494 440090**

Course type: Certificated Project Manager (competency-based certification scheme)

Appendix C References and further reading

Adaire, J. (1990) *Understanding Motivation*, Talbart & Adaire Press, London.

Birchall, D.W. and Newcomb, R. (1985) 'Developing project management skills', *Journal Metals and Materials*, July, pp. 439–441,

Boddy, D. (1993) 'Managing change in changing times', *Management Science Journal,* October.

de Bono, E. (1991) *I Am Right You Are Wrong*, Penguin Books, London.

Dawson, S. (1988) *Analysing Organisations,* Macmillan Education, London.

Hollins, G. and Hollins, B. (1991) *Total Design,* Pitman, London

Lock, D. (1992) *Project Management,* 5th edn, Gower, Aldershot.

Lock, D. (ed.) (1994), *Handbook of Management,* 2nd edn, Gower, Aldershot.

Harrison, F.L. (1992) *Advanced Project Management,* 3rd edn, Gower, Aldershot.

Harrison, F.L. (1988) *Conflict, Power and Politics in Project Management.* Presented at Conception to Completion, 9th World Congress on Project Management, 1988.

Haynes, M.E. (1994) *Project Management,* Kogan Page, London.

Kezsbom, D. (1992) 'Re-opening Pandora's Box', *Industrial Engineering,* May.

McManus J.J. (1994) *Resisting Change,* Lakewood Research Publishing, Minneapolis.

McManus J.J. (1995) *An Implementation Guide on How to Re-engineer Your Business,* Stanley Thornes, Cheltenham.

Peters, T. and Waterman, R. (1982) *In Search of Excellence,* Harper & Row, New York.

Prigl, J. and Stoldt, S. (1990) *Implementing Strategic Project Management at Mercedes-Benz AG, Car Division.* Presented at Managing by Projects, 10th International World Congress, 1990.

Reiss, G. (1992) *Project Management Demystified,* E&FN Spon, London.

Rosenthal, S.R. (1992) *Effective Product Design and Development,* Business One Irwin, Homewood, Ill.

Senge, P.M. (1994) *The Fifth Discipline,* Century Business Books, London.

Stitt, F. (1992) *Project Management Check Lists,* Van Nostrand Reinhold, New York.

Thamhain, H.J. and Wilemon, D.L. (1977) 'Leadership, conflict and program management effectiveness', *Sloan Management Review,* Vol. 19, No. 1.